LAKE BLED TRAVEL GUIDE 2024

Discover the Ultimate Alpine Gem of Slovenia: Your Updated, Pocket-sized Manual to Top tourist Attractions, Fun outdoor activities, Culture, and Hidden Gems.

ERIC BOARD

LAKE BLED TRAVEL GUIDE 2024

All rights reserved. No part of this publication may be reproduced, distributed, or transmitted in any form or by any means, including photocopying, recording, or other electronic or mechanical methods, without the prior written permission of the publisher, except in the case of brief quotations embodied in critical reviews and certain other noncommercial uses permitted by copyright law.

Copyright © by [ERIC BOARD] 2024

Table of Content

Chapter 1: Introduction
An Overview of Lake Bled
The Reasons to Visit Lake Bled
What Sets Lake Bled Apart from Other Lakes

Chapter 2
Getting To Lake Bled
Getting from Ljubljana to Lake Bled:
How To Get To Lake Bled From LJUBLJANA AIRPORT

Chapter 3
Accommodations Options in Lake Bled (Top Hotels)
Luxury Hotels in Lake Bled
Cheap Accommodation In Lake Bled
Private Accommodation In Lake Bled

Chapter 4
Exploring Lake Bled
20 Top things to do in Lake Bled that will leave you in Great Wonder including: Top

Attractions, Fun Outdoor Activities (Both Summer, and Winter).

Chapter 5
Culinary Delights (Top Dishes to Savor in Lake Bled)
Top Restaurants in Bled

Chapter 6
Culture and History
Brief History of Lake Bled
Folklore and Traditions at Lake Bled

Chapter 7
Local Museums in Lake Bled
Events and Festivals at Lake Bled

Chapter 8
Practical Travel Tips
The best time to visit Lake Bled
Packing Tips:
Currency and Payment Information in Lake Bled

Chapter 9

Day Trips from Lake Bled and Nearby Destinations
Lake Bohinj
Vršič Pass
Radovljica
Brda
Vintgar Gorge

Chapter 10
Shopping Places in Lake Bled

Chapter 11
Nightlife in Bled
Top Bars in Bled that will give you an Awesome Nightlife Experience

Chapter 12
6 DAYS ITINERARY
Safety and Emergency Information at Lake Bled
Basic Phrases
Conclusion

Chapter 1: Introduction

An Overview of Lake Bled

Lake Bled is a treasure that is tucked in the heart of Slovenia, and we would like to welcome you to its lovely domain. This chapter offers a wonderful introduction to Lake Bled, which is characterized by its stunning environment, tranquil waters, and culturally and historically significant heritage. Learn about the past that has played a role in the formation of this picture-perfect location, and get an understanding of the reasons why it continues to capture the hearts of tourists from all over the globe.

The Reasons to Visit Lake Bled

For what reasons is Lake Bled an absolute must-see destination? This section delves into the one-of-a-kind experiences and attractions that are responsible for attracting tourists to its attractions. A tapestry of natural beauty and cultural treasures that promises an unforgettable vacation can be found in Lake Bled. From the famous Bled Castle, which is set on a rock, to the peaceful island that is ornamented with a quaint church, Lake Bled provides a wide variety of attractions.

What Sets Lake Bled Apart from Other Lakes

Find out more about the unique qualities that make Lake Bled stand out from other lakes. Whether it's the traditional Pletna boat journeys to Bled Island, the beautiful Vintgar Gorge, or the gorgeous background of the Julian Alps, discover the factors that contribute to the uniqueness of Lake Bled. Uncover the fascination that has made this place a timeless retreat for visitors seeking solitude and natural magnificence.

As you go on your trip through the introduction, let the spirit of Lake Bled's beauty and charm guide the way for a vacation experience full of discovery, relaxation, and enchantment that only this Slovenian treasure can bring.

Chapter 2

Getting To Lake Bled

Slovenia's tiny size makes it easy to move around it. Explore the most efficient methods of how to go to Lake Bled, the alpine gem of the nation.

Slovenia is quite tiny, which means it is pretty simple to access most sections of the nation. Bled is not an outlier with a position in the middle of Slovenia, which means there are many viable methods to get here. Let's look at the finest.

YOU CAN REACH BLED:

By Bus

Because it's a major tourist site, Bled has an above-average volume of buses traveling there each day. There's at least one leaving every hour from Ljubljana, taking a little more than an hour to get there. Some buses also have stops at Ljubljana Airport.

By Train

Bled has two train stations: Lesce-Bled and Bled Jezero.. Both stations are roughly 4 kilometers from the city core, thus we suggest you hire a cab to reach your ultimate destination from there. We prefer the train to Lesce-Bled as it is quicker, you don't need to exchange trains on the way, and you can also take a bus to go to the city center.

By automobile,

The simplest method to travel to Bled is. There's a freeway for most of the journey, save for the final 10 minutes to the city core. It takes roughly 45 minutes to get there from Ljubljana. Follow the highway to the northwest towards Kranj and beyond it for roughly 35 minutes. Exit the highway at Lesce and travel for another 10 minutes, following the numerous signs for Bled

By Plane

Ljubljana Airport Bled is about a 20-minute drive from the Ljubljana Airport. Some of the hotels provide airport shuttle service. Alternatively, we propose you hire a cab or jump on one of the numerous buses that travel in the same direction.

Other nearby airports:

Venice (Marco Polo) Airport is 130 km from Bled Venice (Treviso) Airport 260 kilometers from Bled Zagreb Airport 200 kilometers from Bled Salzburg Airport 230 kilometers from Bled

Getting from Ljubljana to Lake Bled:

Getting from Ljubljana to Lake Bled is fairly straightforward since the two sites are so near. The bus travel from Ljubljana to Lake Bled will cost roughly 1 hour and 20 minutes. Your best choice is to travel with Alpetour, operating a bus hourly. Arriva Slovenia (5 times a day) and Flixbus (daily) are alternative possibilities.

Another alternative is to take a day trip from Ljubljana to see Lake Bled, although Lake Bled is worth more travel time than that.

How To Get To Lake Bled From LJUBLJANA AIRPORT

The bus is the simplest method to travel to Lake Bled from Ljubljana Airport. You will discover multiple bus stops near the airport exit, where you have to hunt for the correct bus stop. There you will discover a schedule. The main transport operator is Arriva and their buses may also be seen on Google Maps to organize your journey. The trip time by bus is roughly 30 minutes from the airport to the major bus station "Bled Union". Therefore, driving directly to Lake Bled from the airport and seeing Ljubljana after Lake Bled is a terrific option to save time on your trip. Another alternative to going from Ljubljana airport to Lake Bled is by taking a cab. This will cost you roughly €50.

Chapter 3

Accommodations Options in Lake Bled (Top Hotels)

Luxury Hotels in Lake Bled

Grand Hotel Toplice - A luxury 5-star accommodation in Lake Bled.

One of the nicest settings in Lake Bled, the Grand Hotel Toplice is the only five-star hotel in Lake Bled. The magnificent hotel provides spectacular views of the Alps and the lake. Bled Straža Ski Lift, Sports Hall Bled, Baby Straza Ski Lift, Bled Castle Bathing Area, Adventure Park Bled, and Bled Castle are all within a 700-meter radius.

All the big rooms and suites are attractively decorated with warm colors and properly equipped. The onsite restaurants provide superb Slovenian and foreign food, while the pubs and cafés serve a selection of beverages.

Guests may enjoy a private beach, boathouse, and swimming pool fed with hot water from a well.

Rowing boats are available for lease, and free WiFi is accessible throughout.

Naturally, the apartments facing the lake offer the nicest view!

Address: Cesta svobode 12, 4260 Bled, Slovenia

Phone:+386 4 579 16 00

Adora Luxury Hotel:Boutique Hotels In Lake Bled:

Previously known as Vila Istra, the Adora Luxury Hotel is one of the top hotels in Lake Bled with amazing views of Bled Island, Lake Bled, and Triglav Mountain.

The core of Bled town is 10 minutes away, while the Straza Mountain is 100 meters away, and the Saza River is 300 meters away. Most attractions are within a mile distance.

Chandeliers grace the ceilings of this gorgeous Lake Bled property, while rooms are well-lighted and furnished with traditionally inspired furnishings. Cozy rooms have free WiFi, refrigerators, workstations, tea/coffee makers, minibars, and basic amenities. Baby cots and family rooms are provided. The suites and deluxe rooms also have dining spaces and balconies with loungers. Perfect for that romantic holiday in Bled!

Address: Cesta svobode 35, 4260 Bled, Slovenia
Phone: +386 31 382 614

Vila Bled

Located on the banks of Lake Bled, Vila Bled was erected in 1947 and was once President Tito's holiday residence. This is one of the Lake Bled luxury hotels that appears like it came directly out of a storybook. The large rooms have cable television, minibars, free WiFi, refrigerators, and other amenities. Mt Straza is 2 km distant, whereas Bled Castle is 1.2 km away.

Free parking is accessible on site, and dogs are also permitted for free

Address: Cesta svobode 18, 4260 Bled, Slovenia

Phone: +386 4 575 37 10

Cheap Accommodation In Lake Bled

You won't find any inexpensive hostels in Lake Bled, but there are guest homes and pensions that are light on the purse.

Pension Zaka

The Pension Zaka bed & breakfast, Lake Bled, is located only 10 meters from the beach of the lake. The Olympic swimming pool is next door, while most of the Lake Bled attractions are within a 2 km radius as it's on the other side of the lake from the town. Supermarket Mercator is 500 meters away.

Rooms at this affordable lodging in Lake Bled are quite big and fully equipped with refrigerators, coffee machines, heating, air conditioning, and TV with satellite channels. The 35 m² comfort room also features a balcony with a view of the Lake.

Free parking is provided on-site, and dogs are allowed at a fee.

Address: Župančičeva cesta 9, 4260 Bled, Slovenia

Phone: +386 40 147 757

Guest House Mlino

This family-run guesthouse in Lake Bled is located near the boat rental. It's also one of the finest spots to stay in Lake Bled if you want to stroll to all the sights.

Rooms at the Guest House Mlino are modest and tidy and feature all conveniences, including free WiFi and mosquito nets. Rooms on the top levels are accessible only via stairs. If you have difficulties ascending, please get in contact with the hotel to request a room on the lower levels once booked.

The onsite Restavracija Penzion Mlino provides Mediterranean, international, and European cuisine, and customers appreciate the breakfast here. Guest House Mlino is one of the top affordable hotels in Lake Bled!

Address: Cesta svobode 45, 4260 Bled, Slovenia

Phone: +386 4 574 14 04

Carman Guest House

Carman Guest House may not be one of the finest hotels in Lake Bled, but it's one of the greatest budget-friendly places to stay in Lake Bled. The cheerful and colorfully designed rooms make you forget their tiny size. They offer an electric kettle, hairdryer, iron, free WiFi, air conditioning, and cable TV.

The 38 m² Comfort Double Room additionally has a balcony, dining room, sitting area, a well-equipped kitchenette, and a private sauna. Perfect for a romantic weekend away.

Free parking is provided onsite.

Address: Cesta svobode 37, 4260 Bled, Slovenia
Phone: +386 51 784 150

Private Accommodation In Lake Bled

There are numerous private lodging alternatives in Lake Bled; here are just a handful to start your search.

Lake Bled Apartments

Lake Bled Apartments appear like an artisan has embellished them. These 120 m² flats may accommodate up to six people in 3 bedrooms. Guests have access to a fully equipped kitchen and free-to-use BBQ. Hypoallergenic bedding and cleaning supplies are supplied, as are free WiFi and parking.

Guests at Lake Bled Apartments enjoy great views of the mountains, lake, and the town of Bled. Bled Castle is 900 meters distant, but the cave beneath Babji Zob is 5 kilometers away. The apartment management may organize hiking, fishing, windsurfing, and other activities for a price.

This property is widely rated as the finest private lodging in Lake Bled.

Apartments Mojca

This individual cottage in Lake Bled is clean and well-furnished. Guests may select from 20 m² rooms or 45 m² or 55 m² flats. The apartments also have free WiFi, a lounge space, a dining area, and a well-equipped kitchen with an oven, hob, coffee machine, toaster, electric kettle, and more.

The whole apartment is wheelchair-accessible, and free parking is offered onsite. Perfect for a quiet stay in Lake Bled! All of the attractions are within a mile walking distance.

Address: Cesta svobode 43, 4260 Bled, Slovenia
Phone: +386 41 845 198

Chapter 4

Exploring Lake Bled

20 Top things to do in Lake Bled that will leave you in Great Wonder including: Top Attractions, Fun Outdoor Activities (Both Summer, and Winter).

Lake Bled is, hands down, one of the most gorgeous sites I've traveled to in Central Europe. Located in the Julian Alps, Lake Bled is one of the numerous lakes in this area that provide a ton of things to do, both outdoors and indoors, from hiking and swimming to visiting historic monuments and indulging in the local cuisine. Within this guide, you will discover a thorough list of the greatest things to do in Lake Bled and all the information you need to enjoy a fantastic time in this magnificent region.

1. Explore Bled Castle

One of the first things you will notice when you arrive in Bled is Bled Castle, an 11th-century medieval fortification erected on a clifftop overlooking the town and the lake. It is one of the most popular landmarks here and one that you should surely not miss.

Due to its spectacular position, Bled Castle provides an unimpeded view of the lake and its surrounds, as well as a museum that showcases the castle's history and antiquities.

It isn't very huge within the castle, with a few museums, cafés, and restaurants spread around the castle courtyard. What will blow your head is the 180° panoramic vista you can see up there. The whole of Lake Bled, as well as all the shoreline villages and the surrounding scenery, can all be viewed from here.

There are various methods to climb up to Bled Castle. The ideal method is to climb from the village, passing by St. Martina Parish Church and zig-zagging your way up the dirt path until you reach the parking area of the castle. It should take you approximately 10 minutes, and you will primarily be under shade most of the time

You may also drive up to Bled Castle and park your vehicle in the castle's approved parking area. There are a ton of parking places here, so you should have no issue driving up here.

Unfortunately, if you want to obtain the greatest view of Lake Bled from Bled Castle, you are going to have to pay the admission price. The admission charge to the castle should be roughly 13 EUR per person, and the castle is accessible from 8 AM to 8 PM every day. The sunset up here may be stunning too, so make sure you schedule your visit properly.

Location: Grajska cesta, 4260 Bled, Slovenia
Opening hours: Various (8 am – 6 or 8 pm)
Adult entrance fee: €11
Phone: +386 4 572 97 82

2. Bled Island (Make a Wish at the Bled Island Church of the Assumption)

If you've seen any images of Lake Bled, you'll undoubtedly know the modest chapel on Bled Island. This is the Church of the Assumption, and it was completed in 1465, with 99 stairs up to its door.

Tradition demands that in marriages happening in the church, husbands must carry their brides up all 99 stairs (talk about a pre-wedding exercise!). Although visiting the island is one of the most popular activities in Lake Bled, it's not something you should miss.

On the island, there's also a renowned wishing bell. Legend has it that there was a lady residing at Bled

Castle whose husband perished in the lake. In her despair, she gathered several of her gold and silver goods and sent them to someone to construct a bell for the little church on the island.

However, the boat carrying the bell also capsized, plummeting the bell to the bottom of the lake.

Upon hearing this, she sold all her things, gave all of the money to construct a new church, and went to Rome and became a nun. Sometime afterward, the Pope heard her tale and created a new bell for the cathedral in her honor.,

Today, as the tale goes, if you ring the Bled church bell three times and make a wish, it will come true.

To reach the island, you'll need to hire a boat or ride a traditional Pletna boat (€14 round trip).

If we think about it further, it is not Lake Bled but rather the little island on it that has become the emblem of Slovenia. The Church of Mother of God was erected for St. Mary and is one of the structures with a historical background on the island that is worth a visit.

When you wander around Lake Bled, you may frequently hear the bells. The noises originate from the island, from the bell tower. Several tales and rumors are known concerning the bell. In one version, while the bell is ringing, you have to wish, whereas according to other accounts, if the bell is rung three times, your wish will be realized. One thing is for sure if you hear the bell, hope for something!

The Poticnica restaurant provides a typical "potica", a form of sweet brioche, to visitors who become hungry during their island visit. Potica is available in numerous tastes. If you go for it, try the walnut variant, which is the most popular.

It takes roughly 2 hours to tour the island. Since the island of Bled is fairly tiny, you will not spend too much time on the island.

Unfortunately, dogs are not permitted on the island, and the island does not have total wheelchair access.

Bled island church costs
- Adults: 6 euro
- Student: 4 euro

- Child: 1 euro
- Family ticket: 12 euro

You may travel to the island by boat (pletna). The island of Bled is available to tourists every day. The exception is if the lake is frozen or the weather is particularly harsh. The island opens at 9 am every day, while the closing time varies on the month. The summer months feature the longest operating hours, with the schedule ranging from 9 am to 7 pm in May through September, while in November through March, the hours are from 9 am to 4 pm, and in April and October, they extend from 9 am to 6 pm.

Address: 4260 Bled, Slovenia

3. Hike Up To Mala Osojnica Viewpoint

One of the highlights of things you can do in Lake Bled is hiking, and one of the greatest hiking routes with a fantastic view over the lake is Mala Osojnica. It is a trekking track that will take you far up in the mountains, enabling you to view the lake in its entirety from above, without flying a drone.

Hiking Mala Osojnica was probably the highlight of my vacation to Lake Bled. The trek begins at the Mala Osojnica trailhead and you can get there simply by strolling along the lakeside walking route from Bled. It should take around 30 minutes of a pleasant stroll before you get to the trailhead.

From the trailhead, it is a straight, steep climb to Mala Osojnica Viewpoint, which should take around 30 minutes maximum. The walk is largely on a dirt track with a few steep roped portions and wooden steps before you get to the viewpoint.

Mala Osojnica is the highest viewpoint of all three perspectives you may trek on this mountain, and it provides you with the greatest view over Lake Bled out of all the viewpoints here.

It is also one of the greatest sites to see the dawn over Lake Bled, and I strongly suggest that you do it if you have the time. Just be sure to plan your trip carefully, since it would take roughly 1 hour to go all the way from Bled Town to the lookout.

From Mala Osojnica, you may also trek to the other two overlooks (Ojstrica and Velika Osojnica) as well, as they are all linked by dirt trails and narrow roads.

I believe Mala Osojnica and Ojstrica give the nicest views over Lake Bled. Mala Osojnica provides you with a wide perspective of the lake, whilst Ojstrica gives you a closer glimpse at the lake and the chapel in the center. One of the nicest things to do at Lake Bled.

Trail Details

- Parking | Parkirišče Velika Zaka | Google Maps
- Trailhead | Mala Osojnica Trailhead | Google Maps
- Distance | 3.7 kilometers lollipop-circuit
- Time Needed | 1:15 – 1:30 hours
- Elevation Gain/Loss | 224 meters
- Difficulty | Moderate
- Minimum Elevation | 479 meters
- Maximum Elevation | 678 meters

Address: Ljubljanska cesta 8, 4260 Bled, Slovenia

Phone: +386 31 838 888

4. Ski (or Slide) the Slopes of Bled

If you're a lover of outdoor activities, one intriguing feature about Bled is that you can hit the slopes year-round.

During wintertime, the neighboring slopes at Straža are accessible and open to skiers of all abilities.

Perhaps one of the craziest things to do in Lake Bled, in the summer, there's a toboggan track where tourists can slide down the same hills!

Either way, if you want to zoom down a hill at breakneck speed, Bled's got you covered, no matter what time of year it is.

5. Take a seat at the affectionate bench located at Ojstrica Viewpoint.

As noted earlier, Ojstrica Viewpoint is another fantastic viewpoint you should climb to for a closer look at Lake Bled and the church in the center of the lake.

From Mala Osojnica, it should take approximately 20 minutes to reach the Ojstrica Viewpoint, or you may climb from Velika Zaka, a village on the western shore of Lake Bled, in roughly the same period.

At Ojstrica, you will see the lake a bit closer and without a steel fence blocking your view, making it a far better position to capture shots of you and the lake than from Mala Osojnica.

There is also a wonderful wooden seat in Ojstrica where you may sit down, rest, and enjoy the magnificent view of the lake. I was there for around 30 minutes without a single person turning up. It was wonderful.

Once you are done, you may continue trekking to Velika Osojnica next or you can make your way down to Velika Zaka, which is a calmer and less busy location to rest and swim for a few hours before coming back to Bled.

Address: 4260 Bled, Slovenia

6. Walk Around The Entire Lake

If you are not so keen on trekking but still want to do something physical, you may alternatively choose a beautiful stroll around the lake from Bled to Velika Zaka and back.

The stroll is really lovely, particularly in the early morning when there aren't many people out and the geese and birds are out in full force. It was so calm and lovely, it is hard to imagine anything better to do than to wander around the lake in the morning.

The full length of the walking trail around the lake is roughly 5.6 km (about 3.5 miles), and it should take you between 1-2 hours to finish. There are various stretches of the walking trail that will take you across the lake on wooden planks, away from the main road, which is fantastic.

There are innumerable things to see and do along the road. You will drive through the picturesque village of Jezero, get an opportunity to trek Mala Osojnica or go for a wonderful swim or kayak in Velika Zaka or wherever along the lake.

The trail is beautifully designed, and you will see practically everything Lake Bled has to offer all in one go. If you have a few hours to spare and the weather is perfect outdoors, you are going to adore it.

7. Kayak Or Swim In The Lake

Another fantastic option to spend time in Lake Bled is to hire a kayak or go for a swim in the lake. Unfortunately, you can't simply swim anywhere you like since you are only permitted to do so in the approved swimming areas found largely around cities and tourist sites.

For the absolute finest swimming site, after spending a few days investigating the lake, I discovered that if you go all the way to the other side of the lake at Velika Zaka, you will find a lot calmer and more tranquil swimming area than on the eastern side of the lake.

There are fewer people on this side of the lake, particularly in the morning, and you will undoubtedly enjoy yourself more. I found the eastern shore of Lake Bled too busy for my taste.

You may also hire a canoe or a kayak and explore the lake as you see fit. There are various sites where you may hire one around the lake, with a normal fee of roughly 20 EUR for an hour and 10 EUR for each additional hour. If you want to keep away from the tourist hordes and spend your day on the lake, this is the way to go.

8. Ziplining in Bled

You will get an adventure park-like experience if you attempt the Bled zipline course. Like rafting, the ropeway is not only a great kid-friendly activity but also a wonderful adrenaline explosion for every member of the family. From the age of 6, children may participate in the program by sliding with their parents or teachers!

The 2-3-hour zipline program costs around 60 euros per person (cheaper for kids) and is available every day of the year, including in winter! On the ropes, you will spend approximately an hour, the remainder of the time strolling between the ropes, as well as a lesson at the beginning, and a shuttle.

The trip is only accessible in English or Slovenian. You may only access the rope park with a guide (typically 2-3 guides/group). Admission must be scheduled in advance but has to be paid for on-site only.

9. Explore Vintgar Gorge

Vintgar Gorge is another fantastic feature of visiting Lake Bled. The canyon is a 1.6-kilometer-long gorge, cut between the spectacular sheer cliffs of Hom and Boršt hills by the great Radovna River.

Along the canyon, you will discover loads of stunning cliffs, lush waterfalls, and a wonderful walking track that extends around the whole valley on wooden bridges. These bridges will carry you to the 13-meter-high Šum River waterfall.

A trip around Vintgar Canyon is one of the highlights of visiting Lake Bled, and you can easily spend roughly 2-3 hours climbing the full length of the canyon and spending some time sitting at the waterfall.

The gorge is around 4 km distant from Bled, and to travel there, you will need to take a shuttle ride from Bled. There is a shuttle service offered by Mamut Slovenia. It operates from Bled Bus Station to Vintgar Gorge and back every hour, and the fee is roughly 10 EUR per person.

With the shuttle transfer, you will have roughly 2 hours to walk the gorge, and the shuttle will pick you up at the end of the path about 2.5 hours after departure.

It is the quickest and most direct method to see the gorge, and I strongly urge that you go for it. Make sure you schedule a time slot from their website beforehand. The slots become booked fairly rapidly, particularly in the summer. One of the nicest things to do at Lake Bled.

Address: Turistično društvo Gorje, Podhom 80, 4247 Zgornje Gorje, Slovenia

Phone: +386 51 621 511

10. Visit Lake Bohinj As A Day Trip

Lake Bohinj is another amazing place to view near Lake Bled. It is situated around 24 kilometers away from Bled and can easily be accessed by the hourly bus that links the two sites together.

Lake Bohinj is significantly closer to the Julian Alps than Lake Bled, and you will surely feel like you are in an alpine lakeside village here, rather than at Lake Bled. The lake is surrounded by majestic Alpine mountain peaks that give a ton of options for hikers and explorers to explore.

If you think the water of Lake Bled is lovely, wait till you see exactly how vibrant the colors of the lake truly are here. The water is very clean and quite welcoming. You may also hire a kayak or a canoe here, or you can simply spend the whole day swimming and sunbathing.

It is also less crowded than Lake Bled and a bit smaller and less bustling. So, if you are seeking a spot to spend a day or two away from Lake Bled, Lake Bohinj is a terrific option.

While there, also make sure to visit the Cerkev Sv. Janeza Krstnika church and walk up to the bell tower for a magnificent view across the lake. From up here, you will realize exactly how big the countryside surrounding Lake Bohinj is.

To go from Bled to Lake Bohinj, you are going to have to grab a bus from Bled Bus Station, which operates every hour from 7:15 AM to 10:20 PM every day. You may view the current bus schedule and purchase the bus ticket straight from the bus terminal in Bled. The bus is run by Arriva, and it may be fairly late at times owing to traffic, so do not sweat it when the bus does not come on time.

Address: 4265 Bohinjsko jezero, Slovenia

11. Visit the Bled Hut

The Bled Hut (Blejska Koča na Lipanci) is a controlled mountain hut situated on the Lipanca mountain pasture above the Pokljuka Plateau in Triglav National Park.

The lovely Bled Cottage (1630 m) was previously a shepherd's cabin. In 1976, the Bled Mountain Society acquired and refurbished the building.

Today, you may visit Blejska Koča na Lipanci virtually all year round. You may have lunch in the hut, or stay overnight (make a reservation in advance).

From the Medvedova Konta Car Park, it's an easy 45-minute stroll along a forest road to Blejska Koča na Lipanci.

While staying in Lake Bled, we strongly suggest taking a half-day journey to Blejska Koča na Lipanci. From the hut, you may continue your journey to the adjacent peaks of Debela peč (2014 m) and Brda (2009 m).

These summits give amazing views of Karma Valley, Rjavina, Mala Rjavina, Luknja Peč, and the Karawanks.

Address: Krnica 99, 4247 Zgornje Gorje, Slovenia
Phone: +386 51 621 021

12. Pokljuka Gorge

The Pokljuka Gorge is about 15 minutes (8 km) from Bled. The hiking path in the gorge is famed for its windowed cave and panoramic bridge. Both sights are worth a visit here and require a half-day stroll.

The most notable navigable tunnel in the Pokljuka Gorge is the massive cave chamber called the Pokljuka Hole. In addition to the two entrances, the hole also features three natural windows, making the rock formation intriguing as well.

The wooden bridge dubbed the 'Galleries of Prince Andrew', is affixed to one of the rock walls of the gorge. You may travel through the gallery, and even the path gets you here.

Address: 4247 Zgornje Gorje, Slovenia

Distance from Bled: 8 km, roughly 15 minutes by vehicle

13. Zelenci Nature Reserve

Zelenci Nature Reserve is a component of Kranjska Gora. Located near the hamlet of Podkoren, this lovely reserve is recognized for its unique lake region, known across Europe. The tint of the water, which is on average 2 meters deep, is green, thus its name (Zelenci means green in Slovenian).

It is also an ideal trip option for families and elders since the national park is situated on a level terrain. About 30 minutes by automobile from Lake Bled on the E61 route.

Address: Podkoren 75, 4280 Gora, Slovenia

Distance from Bled: 42 km / about 35 minutes by vehicle

14. Vogel Mountain and Cable vehicle

If you want to climb to reach the clouds, go up the Vogel Mountain. If you don't want to accomplish all this on your own, pick the Vogel cable car, which takes you up to 1,535 meters.

For fans of alpine scenery, we certainly suggest the program, which is less than a 30-minute drive away. Of course, there are lots of chances for hiking and excursions here, and if you simply want to rest, you can also enjoy a wonderful picnic here with a good book. The perfect daily regimen for mountain enthusiasts.

Distance from Bled: 30 minutes by automobile (above Lake Bohinj)

Location: Ukanc 6, 4265 Bohinjsko Jezero, Slovenia

The Vogel is not only famed for its alpine ambiance, but it is also widely known to skiers since it functions as a ski paradise in winter.

15. Mezica Mine: Underground Kayaking

An unusual and unique experience is the kayak tour of the Mexican mine. Surprisingly, within the mine, which is approximately a 1.5-hour drive from Bled, there is a potential for cave kayaking - of course only on a guided tour.

As part of the program, you will be brought from Bled to the Mezica Cave and mine via transfer. The mine presently solely works as a museum. Here you have the option to test out the train used in the mine, view the exhibits, and kayak in the canals. Please be aware that the museum is not open on Mondays.

The full-day package with a guide and transport from Bled is roughly 100 euros per person.

Unfortunately, the package is not one of the cheapest programs, you can also obtain 3 rafting or canyoning excursions at this price. Therefore, we propose the program to people who have previously tried other sports and wish to try something new.

Address: Glančnik 8, 2392 Mežica, Slovenia

Phone: +386 2 870 01 80

16. Try The Delicious Bled Cream Cake

One of the most wonderful local delicacies you have to taste here is the scrumptious Bled Cream Cake, which is offered at Caffe Peglez'n, among other cafes and restaurants surrounding Lake Bled.

What is so amazing about Bled Cream Cake is the layers that make up the cake. Starting with the base layer, you will discover the wonderful golden crispy crust formed from butter dough, followed by a huge portion of soft, delightful vanilla cream and whipped cream before finishing it off with another layer of crispy crust and a generous sprinkling of icing sugar.

The combination of these layers provides some of the best cakes you will taste all year. Caffe Peglez'n, which is a tiny adorable outdoor café near Bled Castle, provides a nice Bled Cake as well as wonderful coffee and beers. It's a nice site to stop by after a long day trekking around Lake Bled.

17. Eat Štruklji at the Kofce Mountain Hut

Though Lake Bled is situated in the Julian Alps, the mountains that form the background of every swoon-worthy Lake Bled shot are the Karawanks (also called Karavankas, Karavanks, Karawanken, and Karavanke).

The Karavanke mountain series is usually overshadowed by its majestic neighbors, particularly the Julian Alps and the Kamnik-Savinja Alps.

However, these mountains are home to several hidden jewels and unique locales, such as Dom na Kocah.

The maintained Dom na Kofcah (1488 m) is situated on a lovely alpine pasture on the southern side of the Košuta range.

This isn't just any hut. This is the greatest spot in Slovenia to enjoy Štruklji, a classic Slovene meal made composed of dough and different varieties of savory, or sweet ingredients.

You may order Štruklji Sirovi (cheese), Štruklj Čokoladni (chocolate), Štruklj Čokolada Malina (chocolate and raspberry), and Štruklj Ajdovi z orehi (buckwheat and walnuts). Our favorite is Štruklji Borovničevi (blueberry).

There are a few methods to get here. The most common ascending path begins at the Matizovec farm (1:35 hours one-way). We began at the Mimo Kapelice trailhead near Jelendol (30 minutes one-way), due to road work.

Before, or after feeding on Štruklji, consider climbing up to Veliki Vrh.

Address to the Kofce Mountain Hut: Podljubelj 237 Planina Kofce, 4290 Tržič, Slovenia
Phone: +386 40 634 144

18. Try Local Cuisine At Central Bled Restaurant

Finally, for those seeking a restaurant to savor local cuisine, I strongly suggest exploring Central Bled Restaurant, a well-loved establishment situated in the heart of the town.. They serve some delicious dishes using local products such as Cevapcici, steaks, and Slovenian sausages.

The pricing is a tad costly, but you know you are getting your money's worth here. The restaurant operates daily from noon until 10 PM. They are packed at dinner time, so make sure to get there early if you want to reserve a table.

Address: Ulica narodnih herojev 3, 4260 Bled, Slovenia

19. Bled bike hiring, Bled bike tour

If you wish to discover the hidden beauties of the region not only on foot but also by bike, hire a bike or pay for a guided trip. Most local guides now provide excursions by electric bike, so you may get to know the surroundings of Bled much more comfortably and swiftly.

If you only want to ride around the lake, you don't need a local guide. You may hire bicycles in Bled. However, if you want to weave your way around gorges, hills, or forests near Bled, we propose that you hire a local guide who will plan the full excursion for you.

The two most popular locations near Bled are the picturesque landscape of the Mostnica Gorge and the Lake District of the Triglav National Park. Both are around a 1-hour drive from Bled, although there are tour operators who also arrange shuttles from the city, so you don't have to drive.

Electric bike tours

Traveling from Bohinj, which is 30 minutes away from Bled, to Mostnica Gorge takes about 6 hours and costs approximately €65. If you're starting from Bled and heading to Triglav National Park, the journey is around 8 hours with an estimated cost of €65.

20. Pericnik Waterfall

With a height of 52 m, Peričnik Waterfall is one of the tallest and best-known waterfalls in Slovenia. The Vrata Valley hosts a pair of waterfalls.

- Upper Pericnik waterfall: 16 meters
- Lower Pericnik waterfall: 52 meters

An approved hiking track from Mojstrana goes to the site. It's important to know that you may go beneath the Lower Pericnik waterfall, going around the cascade - a great and thrilling experience!

- **Address: 4281 Mojstrana, Slovenia**
- Distance from Bled: appr. 30 minutes
- Parking: €3
- Hike: appr. 15 minutes
- Difficulty: ⅖

Pericnik waterfall hiking path

Head to the town of Mojstrana, from where the excursion will commence. 4 kilometers from the village you will discover the lodge Koca pri Pericniku, where you may park. The big waterfall can already be seen from the parking lot. Before you depart, don't forget to pay the parking charge at the chalet. You will be asked for roughly 3-4 euros for parking. Have cash with you too.

The hiking track will start close to the wooden bridge. You will reach the waterfall in around 15-20 minutes and the first part of the excursion will walk up a difficult slope. By the time you realize it, you've already arrived at the waterfall. The route is hard to damage since you will see the waterfall.

Chapter 5

Culinary Delights (Top Dishes to Savor in Lake Bled)

When it comes to culinary pleasures, Lake Bled provides a magnificent selection of delicacies that represent the rich Slovenian gourmet culture. As you tour the picturesque lakeside and its surrounding surroundings, don't miss the chance to indulge in these great meals that reflect the distinct tastes of the region:

- **Blejska Kremna Rezina (Bled Cream Cake)**: - A culinary marvel and a must-try dessert. Layers of delicate crust, vanilla custard, and whipped cream make this renowned cake a delicious pleasure. Enjoy it in one of the lakeside cafés with a wonderful view.

- **Pletenka:-** A typical Slovenian braided pastry that's both sweet and fulfilling. Often eaten for breakfast or as a snack, Pletenka is a lovely treat with a cup of coffee or tea.
- **Štruklji:** - A savory delicacy that comes in numerous varieties, Štruklji often comprises folded dough filled with cottage cheese, walnuts, or other delightful ingredients. Served either baked or boiled, it's a cozy and tasty alternative.
- **Jota:** - A substantial stew filled with sauerkraut, beans, potatoes, and different meats, Jota is a classic cuisine that warms the soul, particularly during the winter months. Its rich taste is a testimony to Slovenia's culinary tradition.
- **Idrijski Žlikrofi:** - Dumplings stuffed with potato, onion, and bacon, Idrijski Žlikrofi are a specialty of the area. Served with a light sauce or melted butter, these dumplings provide a flavor of Slovenian comfort cuisine.

- **Trout from Lake Bled:** - Indulge in the fresh catch of the day with locally sourced trout from Lake Bled. Grilled or pan-fried, this meal lets you taste the flavors of the crystal-clear waters that surround the lake.
- **Pohorski Lonec:** - A substantial meat and vegetable stew, Pohorski Lonec is a full and flavorsome meal that epitomizes the strong essence of Slovenian cuisine. It's a fantastic option after a day of enjoying the outdoors.
- **Buckwheat Žganci:-** Buckwheat porridge that may be served as a side dish or a main entrée, commonly accompanied by a variety of toppings such as sauerkraut, mushrooms, or meat. A clean and nutritious alternative for people seeking traditional Slovenian food.

Embark on a gastronomic excursion around Lake Bled and sample these outstanding dishes that capture the variety and wonderful flavors of Slovenian cuisine. Whether you have a sweet craving or prefer savory delicacies, Lake Bled offers something to tempt every pallet.

Top Restaurants in Bled

Vila Bled Restaurant

Anyone captivated with the former Yugoslav dictator Tito, or who simply wishes to eat as opulently as him, could ease around the lake away from the throng to the magnificent Vila Bled, where he is known to have taken his loves. Tito's enormous Bled home reclines grandly back from the lake in its exquisite grounds. Best to eat on the patio with the magnificent views - watch out for fresh Lake Bohinj fish and truffles from Istria in the south. Their collection contains some excellent wines from Slovenia's Vipava Valley too. Ask gently and they may even let you visit Tito's old desk upstairs and the gigantic socialist-era paintings.

Address: Cesta svobode 18, 4260 Bled, Slovenia

Phone: +386 4 575 37 10

Gostilna Pri Planincu

This crazy gostilna (gostilna is generally translated as 'inn') is great for your first night. If you want to plunge yourself into the rich realm of Slovenian cuisine dig into game dishes in rich sauces and struklji, a creamy, doughy local favorite. The flip side of this inn appears with its pizza, which provides good pies with a choice of over 20 toppings as a less cultural option. They know what they're doing and they should do — this characterful bolthole has been feeding hungry locals and travelers alike since 1903. It mimics the Slovenian hosting of old, with an interior overflowing with bric-a-brac, including, weirdly, motorcycles hanging from the ceiling.

Address: Grajska cesta 8, 4260 Bled, Slovenia
Phone: +386 4 574 16 13

Vila Preseren

Named after Slovenia's Robert Burns you may find yourself coming over all lyrical at this beautiful retreat. Dine on the terrace by the lake and you can just about touch that glacier water. Enjoy Slovenian classics and good steaks, accompanied with wine from Slovenia's burgeoning Goriska Brda area (think Tuscan wines and comparable surroundings), before topping off your meal with Bled's delightfully creamy dessert masterpiece - kremsnita. The structure itself is suitably lovely, going back to the 19th century. If you have a very wonderful night you may remain here too. The main negative is service might be intermittent, but the sights typically make up for it.

Address: Veslaška promenada 14, 4260 Bled, Slovenia
Phone: +386 4 575 25 10

Park Cafe

You have to sample Bled's most renowned sweet confection, the kremsnita. This excessively calorific concoction is simply a large slab of vanilla custard and cream bordered by flaky pastry and topped with icing sugar. The café asserts itself as a Bled trailblazer, having served here since 1953.. Savor a slice with a local latte (bela kava) and enjoy panoramic views of the lake. The sleek crew provides light meals too - you couldn't handle anything heavier if you're ending up with Kremsnita!

Address: Cesta svobode 10, 4260 Bled, Slovenia

Phone: +386 4 579 18 18

Bled Castle Restaurant

Were this restaurant merely cranking out an international buffet cuisine it would still be worth eating there for the views over Lake Bled. As a bonus, it's one of Bled's top restaurants under the innovative guidance of chefs Luka Jezersek and Ana Sustersic. Think Istrian truffles with Istrian pasta, or chicken packed with shrimps accompanied with buckwheat and asparagus. Note from 6 pm they only serve their multi-course tasting meals. You may indulge yourself with complementary wines. Entry to the castle is included if you're enjoying a full lunch.

Address: Grajska cesta 61, 4260 Bled, Slovenia

Phone: +386 4 620 34 44

Julijana

The most luxurious of the Grand Hotel Toplice's restaurants, the exclusive Julijana, just seats 20 diners inside with a further 20 covers enticing on their lake-view patio. At the helm is eccentric head chef Simon Bertoncelj, who toys with you by combining classic Slovenian cuisine with a dose of inventiveness. A noteworthy dish is grilled Adriatic langoustine tails, laced with shiitake cream and sudachi sauce, with glazed wide beans and mixed lentils, held together by a langoustine foam scented with lemongrass. Bertoncelj performs miracles with the freshwater fish zander, cooking it in butter with a chardonnay sauce, new potatoes with spider crab, and fresh horseradish. Almost as magnificent as those vistas.

Address: Cesta svobode 12, 4260 Bled, Slovenia
Phone: +386 4 579 10 00

Finefood Brec

Fancy fancy dining someplace in classy environs with a piano tinkling away in the background? You just discovered it. From a brilliantly performed traditional

Slovenian beef sou to a hefty back of wild boar, buckwheat dumplings, and cranberry sauce, they get everything right there. Their steaks are famed too - the tastiest come topped with freshly shaved black truffle. Brec also provides tasting meals - the greatest way to experience their entire abilities at work. A patio pours outdoors in summer; their well-picked wines by the glass flow all year.

Address: Želeška cesta 15, 4260 Bled, Slovenia
Phone: +386 40 366 017.

Penzion Mlino

This characterful old-timer nestle is situated around a calmer portion of Lake Bled overlooking a tiny bathing beach. It's cozy and pleasant, set in a classic structure slightly back from the river. Slovenian foods are done perfectly, such as venison spiced up with cranberry sauce, wild boar combined with a dried plum sauce, and a substantial game goulash. Locally caught and smoked fish tempts too, as do some crisp local white wines. A decent fireplace makes things comfortable in the colder months. They have rooms too.

Address: Cesta svobode 45, 4260 Bled, Slovenia

Phone: +386 4 574 14 04

Pr' Povsin

If you seek a true sample of Slovenia's rural hinterland this retreat reclines between Alpine meadows and luscious orchards only 2km from Lake Bled. Don't anticipate pristine tablecloths and silver service. Do anticipate super fresh true handcrafted meals employing ultra local ingredients, the type that Slovenians appreciate away from visitors on a Sunday afternoon. Pungent cheese, air-dried ham, and cured meats feature, all washed down with the local firewater brandy. Much of what you consume is grown right here on their farm. Most diners stay over, but you don't have to.

Address: Selo pri Bledu 22, 4260 Bled, Slovenia

Chapter 6

Culture and History

Brief History of Lake Bled

Prehistoric Origins

Lake Bled, located in the Julian Alps of Slovenia, with a history that transcends millennia. Traces of early human settlements near the lake stretch back to ancient times. The area was undoubtedly occupied by several tribes, leaving behind artifacts that hint at the early human presence in this gorgeous setting.

Medieval Bled Castle:

The medieval history of Lake Bled is entwined with the building of Bled Castle, built on a rock overlooking the lake. Builtin the 11th century, the castle acted as a defensive bastion against invasions and played a crucial role in the region's government. Over the years, Bled

Castle developed, reflecting the architectural styles and strategic necessities of numerous governing powers.

The Pilgrimage Church of the Assumption:

On Bled Island, the Church of the Assumption, with its famous stairs and bell tower, has been a center of pilgrimage since the 15th century. Legend has it that the chapel was established on the site of an old pagan temple dedicated to the Slavic goddess of love. The picturesque Pletna boats, unique to Lake Bled, have carried tourists to the island for decades.

From Habsburg Rule to Yugoslav Era:

Lake Bled became a famous summer getaway throughout the 19th century under the Habsburg Empire. The nobility erected homes along the shoreline, adding to the region's cultural and social life. In the 20th century, Lake Bled became part of the Kingdom of Yugoslavia. The foundation of the Yugoslav state introduced new dynamics, although the tranquil beauty of Lake Bled continued to draw tourists.

Post-Independence Renaissance:

Following Slovenia's independence in 1991, Lake Bled had a rebirth as a tourist attraction. The area embraced sustainable tourism, conserving its natural beauty while attracting people from across the globe. Today, Lake Bled serves as a symbol of Slovenia's cultural legacy, merging medieval history with the attractiveness of its lakeside attraction.

Lake Bled's history is a riveting saga of human settlement, medieval fortifications, religious pilgrimage, and the metamorphosis into a modern-day sanctuary for tourists seeking both cultural richness and natural grandeur. As tourists explore the shoreline, Bled Castle, and the legends engraved in each stone, they become part of the everlasting saga that is Lake Bled's history.

Folklore and Traditions at Lake Bled

The Legend of the Sunken Bell:

One of the most charming traditions at Lake Bled is on the Church of the Assumption on Bled Island. According to local mythology, a young widow from Bled lived in despair following her husband's death. To commemorate his memory, she chose to gift a bell to the island's church. While carrying the bell across the lake, a storm ensued, drowning the boat and the bell. The sad widow subsequently sought peace by ringing the "Wishing Bell" in the church's tower, hoping that every toll would lessen the pain of her departed love. Today, tourists continue the custom by expressing a wish and ringing the bell, listening as its melodious melody resonates over the lake.

Pletna Boat Tradition:

The characteristic Pletna boats, with their colorful awnings and experienced oarsmen, play a significant part in Lake Bled's traditions. These historic wooden boats have been ferrying guests to Bled Island for generations. The talent of the Pletna boatmen is typically handed down through generations, establishing a bloodline of persons who navigate the pristine waterways with precision. The act of rowing tourists to the island has become a beloved tradition, retaining the distinctive attractiveness of these wooden watercraft.

Wedding Traditions on Bled Island:

Bled Island is a significant and picturesque site for marriages, and countless traditions surround this unique ceremony. According to local traditions, the man must carry his wife up the 99 stairs leading to the Church of the Assumption. Legend has it that if the groom completes this duty, a long and happy marriage is ensured. Additionally, newlyweds typically ring the Wishing Bell jointly, expressing their wishes and desires for a good life together.

St. Martin's Day Celebrations:

St. Martin's Day on November 11th is commemorated with a distinct local custom. On this day, Lake Bled is "lowered" by around 10 meters as part of a maintenance routine for the dam. This yearly occasion is followed by celebrations, including a symbolic "burial of the lake" ritual. Locals and tourists congregate to observe this custom, commemorating the changing seasons and the onset of winter.

Lake Bled's mythology and customs give a layer of charm to the already stunning scenery. Visitors may immerse themselves in these practices, whether by casting a wish at the Wishing Bell, experiencing the expert rowing of a Pletna boatman, or watching the symbolic events that mark the passage of time in this Slovenian jewel.

Chapter 7

Local Museums in Lake Bled

- **Bled Castle Museum**: - Housed inside the walls of Bled Castle, this museum provides a thrilling tour through the medieval history of Lake Bled. Exhibits include antiques, weapons, and interactive exhibits that give insights into the castle's role and the region's growth throughout the years. **Highlights**: Medieval armor and weapons, historical relics, interactive exhibits on castle life.
  Address: Grajska cesta 61, 4260 Bled, Slovenia
  Phone: +386 4 572 97 82

- **Museum of Apiculture:** Located near Lake Bled, this museum pays tribute to Slovenia's historic beekeeping culture. Visitors may explore

the world of bees, learn about traditional beekeeping techniques, and understand the important function of bees in the local ecology.
Highlights: Beekeeping gear, historical beekeeping exhibitions, live observation hive.
Address: Linhartov trg 1, 4240 Radovljica, Slovenia

- **Upper Carniola Museum** – Jesuit Collar Collection: Situated in the center of Bled, this museum shows a rare collection of Jesuit collars. The exhibitions give insights into clerical clothing and the historical ties between religious organizations and the area.
Highlights: Jesuit collar collection, historical religious antiques.

Exploring these museums gives a varied knowledge of Lake Bled's cultural legacy, from its medieval roots to the complex customs and technical breakthroughs that have defined this Slovenian beauty.

Events and Festivals at Lake Bled

- **Bled Days (Blejski Dnevi):** - A bustling festival that normally takes place in July, Bled Days provides a range of cultural activities, concerts, and plays. The celebration finishes with a stunning fireworks show over Lake Bled, creating a celebratory mood for residents and tourists alike.

- **Bled Festival (Bledski Festival):** This annual cultural event, held in September, brings together artists, musicians, and performers from diverse genres. The program comprises classical and contemporary music concerts, theatrical performances, and art exhibits, complementing the cultural tapestry of Lake Bled.

- **Bled Days of Adventure (Dnevi Pustolovskega Turizma):** Adventure lovers meet in Lake Bled for a fascinating festival that promotes numerous outdoor activities. From water sports and hiking to adrenaline-pumping excursions, Bled Days of Adventure emphasizes the region's natural beauty and leisure choices.

- **International Regatta (Mednarodna Regata):** Lake Bled's International Regatta, normally held in May, draws rowing enthusiasts from across the globe. The event incorporates competitive rowing races, bringing a lively and competitive attitude to the peaceful waters of Lake Bled.

- **Bled Castle Wine Tasting (Vinski Grad Bled):** Wine lovers and fans congregate at Bled Castle for a unique wine-tasting experience. This event, generally hosted in the castle's gorgeous courtyard, offers guests to drink a range of

Slovenian wines while enjoying panoramic views of Lake Bled.

- **Okarina Ethno Festival**:Celebrating international music and cultural variety, the Okarina Ethno Festival takes place in Lake Bled, bringing together musicians and artists from diverse corners of the globe. The festival normally happens in July and presents a rich tapestry of musical acts.

- **Rowing World Championships:**Lake Bled has been a prominent location for international rowing competitions, including the Rowing World Championships. This tournament gathers elite rowing competitors and gives spectators exciting races against the background of the picturesque Julian Alps.

Participating in these events and festivals enables tourists to experience the active cultural and recreational scene of Lake Bled, creating lasting memories against the background of its stunning natural surroundings.

Chapter 8

Practical Travel Tips

The best time to visit Lake Bled

The Guide to Lake Bled picks of ideal time to visit, well, anytime!

Lake Bled is an all-year-round destination. It all depends on what you want to do, however, if you are in the region and assume it is "out of season" you couldn't be more incorrect! I have gone there in the middle of Winter and discovered that the snowy scenery creates a fairy tale sense that is fantastic

If you are planning a vacation, however, then here is the Guide to Lake Bled run down of what to anticipate.

- **Summer** - May to September are considered as Summer in Lake Bled. You will find the largest number of people during this timeframe, but with temperatures resting between 25° and 30°C, it is a lovely time to be enjoying the lake. Unfortunately, July and August are not only the warmest months but also the wettest.

- **Autumn** — September to November – Less people and temperatures about 18°C, tend to be more around 12°C in November. Still a lovely time of year for trekking, but not so much swimming.
- **Winter** — December to February – Temperatures vary from roughly 7°C to below 0. Although it's chilly, it can also be incredibly attractive with snow a common occurrence. You will have no hassles with crowds, and costs are cheaper. Sometimes the Lake freezes over, so ice skating is feasible!
- **Spring** – March to May – Things begin to warm up a bit in Spring at Lake Bled, and as the snow melts in the neighboring hills, trekking becomes more accessible. Temperatures start early in Spring at approximately 12°C, but coming into May you can anticipate it to be more around 23°C.

Average Temperatures:

- Spring: 8°C to 20°C (46°F to 68°F)
- Summer: 15°C to 27°C (59°F to 81°F)
- Fall: 6°C to 18°C (43°F to 64°F)
- Winter: -5°C to 6°C (23°F to 43°F)

Packing Tips:

1. **Clothing:-**

- Spring and Fall: Layers, including a light jacket, since temperatures may change.
- Summer: Light and airy clothes, swimwear, and sunscreen.
- Winter: Warm layers, waterproof jacket, and cold-weather accessories.

2. **Footwear:** - Comfortable walking shoes for visiting the lakefront and hiking paths.
Winter boots if visiting during the winter seseason.

3. **Outdoor Gear:-** Hiking gear if you want to explore the neighboring trails.Swimsuit for lake activities throughout the warmer months.Winter sports equipment if coming in winter.

4. **Accessories:** - Sunscreen, sunglasses, and a hat for sun protection. Umbrella or rain jacket for unexpected rain showers. Bring a camera to capture the breathtaking scenery.

5. **Travel Essentials:** - Passport, travel insurance, and any essential travel paperwork. Power adaptor for electrical gadgets.Portable charger for lengthy outdoor activities.

6. **Health and Safety:** - Any required medicines and a basic first aid kit. Hydration pack or reusable water bottle for outdoor activities.

7. **Cultural Considerations:-** Modest clothes for trips to churches and cultural places.Respectful clothing for fine dining or cultural activities.

By preparing carefully and considering the seasonal weather differences, you can make the most of your

Lake Bled experience, whether you're exploring the outdoors, experiencing cultural activities, or just resting by the quiet lakeside.

Currency and Payment Information in Lake Bled

Currency:

- The official currency of Slovenia, including Lake Bled, is the Euro (€). It is advisable to carry some cash for modest transactions, since not all establishments may take cards, particularly in more distant regions or local markets.

Payment Methods:.

- Credit and Debit Cards: Major credit and debit cards (Visa, MasterCard, Maestro) are frequently accepted at hotels, restaurants, and major stores in Lake Bled. However, it's advised to bring some cash for smaller places and local markets.
- ATMs: - ATMs are commonly accessible in Lake Bled, giving a quick option to withdraw Euros.

Check with your bank ahead to see if your card will operate overseas and to learn about any costs related to foreign transactions.

Contactless Payments:-

- Contactless payments are becoming increasingly widespread in Slovenia. Many locations, particularly in metropolitan areas, allow contactless card payments for extra convenience.

Currency Exchange: -

- Currency exchange facilities are accessible in bigger cities and tourist locations, including Lake Bled. However, prices may fluctuate, so it's important to check rates or withdraw cash from ATMs for a more advantageous exchange.

Mobile Payments: -

- Mobile payment solutions, such as Apple Pay and Google Pay, are increasingly accepted in select places. Check with your bank and the nearby establishments to see whether they offer mobile payments.

Tipping:

- Tipping is usually appreciated in Slovenia but is not mandatory. In restaurants, it's typical to round up the bill or give a tip of roughly 5-10%, depending on the service. Tipping is also frequent in cafés and for other services.

Note: Always advise your bank about your trip dates and destination to prevent any complications with card transactions overseas. It's also important to have a variety of payment options to ensure you're prepared for diverse circumstances.

Chapter 9

Day Trips from Lake Bled and Nearby Destinations

Lake Bohinj

There's so much to do in and around Slovenia's biggest permanent lake. Lake Bohinj is about 15 miles (25 km) southwest of Lake Bled. You can swiftly travel to Lake Bohinj in approximately 30 minutes; believe us; you'll want to spend the entire day there! The lake, shaped by glaciers, spans 2.6 miles (4.2 km) in length and reaches a maximum width of 0.62 miles (1 km).

A 7.4-mile (12 km) route extends around the boundary of Lake Bohinj. Walking around the lake is a great pastime for individuals who wish to appreciate the beauty and calm of the surrounding environment. If you prefer to walk the whole lake, expect anything from 3.5 to 5 hours. Most visitors walk counterclockwise around the lake, beginning at the Church of St John, near the stone bridge at the lake's southeast end. 14th-century frescoes decorate this more than the 700-year-old church. You'll enjoy rocky, wooded, and meadowed landscapes along the walk surrounding Lake Bohinj.

Lake activities encompass swimming, canoeing, kayaking, and stand-up paddleboarding. Nearby lies Savica Waterfall, Slovenia's most popular waterfall. The path to the falls is short, around 20-30 minutes from the paid parking lot. And although short, it's an uphill journey through a dense forest. There is a nominal admission charge (3 euros per person) to view the waterfall. Another activity in Bohinj to consider, if you remain until the sun goes set, is stargazing! Due to the absence of city lights, the black night sky near Bohinj is spectacular. For stunning views of the Bohinj area, you have three exhilarating alternatives. Your first choice is to ride the Vogel Cable Car close to a mile (1,535 m) above the valley bottom. This option is good for persons with mobility challenges since strollers and wheelchairs are welcome. Once reaching the summit, you'll have access to several wonderful hiking and bike paths, or you may soak in the vistas.

Your second choice for peak views is to travel the twisty journey to Koprivnik Village. It should take you around 25 minutes from Bohinj. Park near the 18th-century parish church and follow instructions to Vodnikov Razglednik (panoramic location). This hard but enjoyable climb should only take around 15 minutes. The vistas of Upper Bohinj Valley and Lake Bohinj from here are well worth the trek! If you're feeling especially courageous, your third choice for breathtaking views over the Bohinj Valley is to jump from a mountain... with a parachute, of course! Paragliding is a popular pastime in this area and no doubt you'll witness a few paragliders gently floating through the sky during your stay in Bohinj.

Address: 4265 Bohinjsko jezero, Slovenia
Drive: Approximately 15.5 mi/25 km | 25-30 minutes
Bus: Operated by Alpetour – Potovalna Agencija, D.O.O. | Departs from Bled Station multiple times

throughout the day | 37-minute travel | Cost is merely a few Euros |
Ride: You may ride between Lake Bled and Lake Bohinj, but remember that there are no specific cycling pathways, and you will be on the main highway with other automobiles and buses.

Vršič Pass

Another alternative for a day excursion from Lake Bled is to drive the Vršič Pass, Slovenia's highest mountain pass. The start of the pass closest to Lake Bled is at the village of Kranjska Gora, a little over a 30-minute drive away.

Vršič Pass is a winding and picturesque road across Triglav National Park, Slovenia's only national park. The park is around 340 square miles (880 square km), making up nearly 3% of the nation!

It's crucial to know that the pass is blocked during the winter months owing to severe snowfall. The route is only available for an average of 7 months a year, so if going around winter, make careful to verify whether the road is open before making this day excursion from Lake Bled.

The Vršič Pass winds in the center of the Julian Alps, and yes, this road winds! With 50 hairpin curves, this trip is not for the faint of heart. The route is small, with two-way traffic ranging from motorbikes to RVs.

Cows, lambs, and other mountain creatures have been known to walk onto the road, so the motorist must be particularly cautious! Each turn is designated with a number (1-50) and the height. Give yourself plenty of time to make stops along the journey to soak in the jaw-dropping splendor of Triglav National Park.

Several suggested stops on the mountain route, including the Russian Chapel (at turn 8), honor the 300 Russian prisoners of war who perished in 1916. These captives were forced to build the road and met their sad fate when they were buried in an avalanche while working on the route. Just beyond turn 16 is a nice halt for magnificent views. It's also a beautiful environment to wander about and have a picnic lunch.

See if you can identify the hole in the mountain, known as the Front Window (Prednje okno), throughout your expedition. The famed Pagan Girl (Ajdovska Deklicacan) rock formation can also be viewed from here, but you'll have an opportunity to go a lot closer at the crest of the pass. At turn 17, you'll notice a vast collection of piled boulders left behind by earlier travelers. Once you reach turn 24, you'll know you've made it to the summit at 5,285 feet (1,611 m)!

The bulk of passengers get off and roam about at the summit. There are various routes you may go to stretch your legs. The most popular walk is a short 15-minute stroll to the mountain hut at Poštarski dom na Vršiču. Along the trail, you will get a closer look at the Pagan Girl rock formation, a famous pagan deity. See if you can spot this interesting structure in the rocks.

Once you're done exploring at the summit, it's all downhill from here... literally! You've got 26 more hairpin twists to go before you reach Trenta. And the turns become a bit tighter from here. The speed limit is unexpectedly 90 km/h (55 mph), but most motorists are a bit more careful and go below the legal speed limit.

At turn 48, look out at the bronze statue of Dr. Julius Kugy, an Italian botanist. He's renowned in the Julian Alps as the father of contemporary alpinism. At turn 50 in Trenta, clap yourself on the back… you just survived driving up and over the Vršič Pass! Enjoy views of the bright blue waters of the Soča River. You may turn around and travel back over the pass to return to Lake Bled or continue and see more of the lovely Triglav National Park.

Address: 5232 Soča, Slovenia

Drive: roughly 25 mi/40 km | 40 minutes | This road includes tolls | This is simply to get to Kranjska Gora, the start of the pass | The pass itself is roughly 15.5 mi/25 km each way | How long it takes you to drive the pass will depend on how frequently you stop to explore and climb

Radovljica

For another quick day excursion from Lake Bled, you'll only need to travel around 10 minutes! The delightful small hamlet of Radovljica is well worth a visit on your journey to Slovenia. Its claim to fame is that it features Slovenia's sole still-existing moat, which goes back to roughly the year 1500.

On Tuesdays, the local tourist information center (located in the Old Town) provides a free walking tour at 10 am. Otherwise, you may pop by the tourist office during business hours to pick up a map of the town and perform your self-guided tour.

The local feature is The Sivic House, a remarkable example of a restored 16th-century gothic-renaissance house. Much of the Old Town center has been retained in the structure and architecture of a 14th/15th-century medieval town.

Seeing the black marble altar at the Church of St Peter is another suggested stop on your tour to Radovljica, in addition to the Chapel of St Edith Stein, which is situated in an ancient German WWII bunker behind the Church of Saint Peter. Edith was a German Jewish philosopher turned nun who perished in the Auschwitz death chambers after the Nazis seized all Catholic Jews in Holland (where she had fled).

The Old Town Plaza features numerous unique galleries, museums, historical buildings, and cafés. So, although the town may be small, there's lots of great stuff to check out. The surrounding country is breathtaking as well, with vistas of the Julian Alps in every direction you look. To the east is the Dežela plain, while to the west is the Sava river valley.

Fun Fact: Radovljica has more sunny days than anyplace else in the Gorenjska area. With it being one of the closest day excursions from Lake Bled, why not explore the sunny town of Radovljica?

Address: 4240 Radovljica, Slovenia
Drive: Approximately five mi/8 km | 10-15 minutes
Bus: Operated by Alpetour – Potovalna Agencija, D.O.O. | Departs from Bled Station multiple times

throughout the day | 14-minute travel | Cost is simply a few Euros
Bike – Approximately five mi/8 km | Small elevation change.

Brda

Do you love wine? If so, you should certainly schedule a visit to the wine area of Brda as one of your day excursions from Lake Bled. (Please note, this is the Municipality of Brda (Goriška Brda), not to be confused with the settlement of Brda near Radovljica.)

The travel to Goriška Brda from Bled will take a little over 2 hours. Depending on whatever route you come, you may even drop into Italy for a few minutes, since the area straddles the Slovenia-Italy border.

If you have a chance to pass Paradiso dei Golosi on your brief journey across Italy, make sure to stop in for some excellent gelato! Even if you don't enjoy wine, Goriška Brda is a wonderful place to explore with picturesque rolling hills and historic villages. Brda refers to 'the country of hills' and has been rightfully termed 'The Tuscany of Slovenia.' Rebula is the area's most popular and unique wine since the grapes required to manufacture this wine are only cultivated within a 40 km radius of the Brda region. Rebula is a pleasant white wine with lemon and green apple flavors. Other popular wine varietals include Cabernet-Merlot blends, Sauvignonasse, a Jakot wine (which is created from the same grapes as the Sauvignonasse), and Merlot, to mention a few.

Dobrovo Castle holds the biggest co-op cellar in Slovenia and is a fantastic site to enjoy some wine sampling. Most wine tastings in Brda take place in people's residences with the homeowner's wine collection.

Note: You must phone ahead to check whether they welcome visitors, so a little pre-planning has to go into your wine-tasting trip in Brda.

As said, there are numerous medieval towns found inside the Brda municipality. Sadly, a substantial chunk of the region's communities was devastated in an earthquake in

1976. However, vestiges of medieval buildings may still be observed across the area.

Several castles and churches, together with the picturesque town of Smartno, date back to the Middle Ages. From its prominent perch on a panoramic hill, Smartno can be seen from pretty much anywhere in Brda.

The church in Smartno, St Martin, is the biggest in Brda and has a bell tower that was previously a defensive tower. Kozano is another little town worth investigating. Its church, St Hieronymus, features a bell tower that stands distinct from the church.

Vipolze and Medana are more attractive towns to explore on your day trip to the wine area of Brda.

Getting from Lake Bled to Brda:

Drive: Approximately 105 mi/170 km | 2 hours | This certainly is your best option, since you will need a vehicle to navigate between the communities in the area

There is no direct bus connection between Lake Bled and the wine area of Brda. With transfers, bus travel will take slightly over 6 hours - not too doable for a day excursion, thus not suggested.
Address:Slovenia

Vintgar Gorge

A day excursion to Vintgar Gorge from Lake Bled is a no-brainer. The two are almost directly next to each other. Well, it's a little over a 10-minute trip (3.3 miles/5.4 kilometers), approximately as lengthy as the journey to RadovljicaYouou could visit Vintgar Gorge and Radovljica on the same day, if you're short on time for day excursions from Lake Bled.

Like Lake Bled, Vintgar Gorge is one of Slovenia's most famous attractions, and it can become quite busy, particularly in the summer months. If you want to beat the crowds, come there early or go much later in the day! By 10 am, the busses have arrived, and throngs of guests will choke the path.

Here's a suggestion: wake up before dawn to witness the sunrise at Lake Bled, then after the sun is up, walk on over to the gorge. You'll be among the first ones there. You may even have the apartment to yourself for a short time.

There is a tiny admission charge (only a few Euros) to access Vintgar Gorge. Worth it!

A 1-mile (1600m) route travels through the gorge and across the Radovna River. The pathway begins as a wooden walkway and soon becomes a nice pebbled path with a few steps. It's a pleasant, family-friendly trek for individuals of all ages. Along the walk, you'll come across a single-arch stone bridge created in 1906 as part of the Bohinj Railway. Here, a human-made dam transports water from the river to the tiny hydroelectric power plant beneath Šum waterfall, Slovenia's tallest river waterfall (43 ft/13 m). Šum waterfall refers to 'noisy falls.' Many people utilize the falls as a turn-around place and go back to the parking lot.

Otherwise, you would need to have planned transportation pick-up at the opposite end of the path.

Walking back toward the entrance to the canyon offers another viewpoint, and you'll have the chance to absorb the majesty of the gorge once again.

Getting from Lake Bled to Vintgar Gorge:
Drive: Approximately 3.7 mi/6 km | 12-15 minutes
Bus – Operated by Alpetour: Potovalna Agencija, D.O.O. | Departs from Bled Station multiple times throughout the day (summer months only) | 9-minute travel | Cost is merely a few Euros
Bike: Approximately 3.7 mi/6 km | Please notice, there are a few hills along this route.
Address: Turistično društvo Gorje, Podhom 80, 4247 Zgornje Gorje, Slovenia

Chapter 10

Shopping Places in Lake Bled

- **Galerija Mikame:** A boutique gallery featuring unique Slovenian crafts, jewelry, and artwork, great for unusual souvenirs.

  Address: Cesta svobode 15, 4260 Bled, Slovenia

- **Art Market Bled:** Held on particular days, this open-air market highlights local artists and craftspeople, selling handcrafted gifts.

  Address: Ljubljanska cesta 15a, 4260 Bled, Slovenia

- **Vila Bled Gift Shop:** Located inside the legendary Vila Bled, this boutique provides excellent souvenirs and gifts, complementing the medieval atmosphere.

  Address: Ljubljanska cesta 4, 4260 Bled, Slovenia

- **Mercator Bled:** A local store where you may buy Slovenian specialties, wines, and snacks to take home.

  <u>Address: Ljubljanska cesta 4, 4260 Bled, Slovenia</u>

- **Bled Cream Cake Boutique:** Satisfy your sweet craving with Bled's famed cream cake, available at this exclusive store.

  <u>Address: Grajska cesta 3, 4260 Bled, Slovenia</u>

- **Čebelarna Čop** - Apiary and Honey Shop: Indulge in locally made honey and honey-based items, a delicious flavor of Lake Bled.

  <u>Address: Brdo pri Lukovici 8, 1225 Lukovica, Slovenia</u>

- **Alpe Adria Artisan:** Discover a range of handmade objects, from pottery to fabrics, produced by local craftsmen.

  Address: Tehnološki park 19, 1000 Ljubljana, Slovenia

- **Bled Farmer's Market:** Open-air market offers fresh vegetables, local cheeses, and handcrafted crafts, creating a colorful shopping experience.
  <u>**Address: Ljubljanska cesta 15a, 4260 Bled, Slovenia**</u>
- **Slaščičarna Zima**: A pastry store where you can get delectable treats and pastries to enjoy on the road or bring back as presents.
  <u>**Address: Grajska cesta 3, 4260 Bled, Slovenia**</u>
- **Bled Fashion Studio**:Trendy clothes and accessories shop featuring a blend of local and foreign designs.
  <u>**Address: Ljubljanska cesta 3, 4260 Bled, Slovenia**</u>.

Whether you're seeking traditional Slovenian crafts, scrumptious sweets, or trendy souvenirs, these shopping destinations in Lake Bled provide a lovely selection of possibilities.

Chapter 11

Nightlife in Bled

Top Bars in Bled that will give you an Awesome Nightlife Experience

Technically Bled is more a town than a city, thus the party scene is not as hectic as in Ljubljana. That nevertheless does not imply that there's no nightlife for you to enjoy. There are a couple of pretty fantastic pubs where you can party hard while basking in the spell-binding ambiance of the lake. The bad news is that all of these establishments shut at 3 am, so it's advisable to start partying a little earlier than normal, particularly if you consider yourself a party animal. Careful however if you want to start outdoors since it's forbidden to drink in public areas, meaning you should keep away from famous tourist sites, such as those near the lake. Also, be cautious not to "drink & drown" as the locals like to phrase it - we don't encourage swimming while you're intoxicated. Ever. Another thing to bear in mind regarding swimming is that it's only allowed in a few specified areas around the lake and nowhere else.

Pub Bled

First on our list is Pub Bled also known by the locals as Troha Bar and one of the greatest party locations in Bled. It's filled virtually every night, with people progressively loosening up and pounding the floor as the celebration advances. Things become even more chaotic once the bar Crawl gets there and the bar fills up to capacity. They have DJs on most evenings and are recognized for their large assortment of mixed beverages and cocktails. You're also able to get a look at the castle if maybe you opt to visit them by day. The gathering is generally a mix of visitors and students.

Address: Ljubljanska cesta 4, 4260 Bled, Slovenia

Kult Klub

Is a spot commonly attended by a more alternative audience. That unfortunately is not the case in peak season when visitors take over, so no concerns about the music being too edgy. Kult is situated on the ground level of the Bled shopping center, just across the street from the lake, and boasts one of the greatest views from the patio. It also regularly holds concerts of diverse genres making it all the more entertaining.

Address: Ljubljanska cesta 4, 4260 Bled, Slovenia

Rock Bar

Is placed immediately next to a hockey rink, viewable from inside the Bar. It features a distinctive rock-inspired atmosphere and as the name says they mostly play rock music. Other than that they also provide a broad assortment of beers.

Address: Ljubljanska cesta 5, 4260 Bled, Slovenia

Art Cafe Bar

A wonderful chill-out establishment with a wide patio facing the lake. The pub is wonderful for lunchtime drinking and on certain evenings may also transform into a terrific party spot. It mainly draws a younger audience, such as students from the Bled School of Business. The decor is beautiful and warm with gold-framed artwork and a wonderful ancient spiral staircase. This is also the meeting spot for Pub Crawls.

Address: Cesta svobode 7a, 4260 Bled, Slovenia

Devil Bar

A considerably darker location, split over 2 stories, with classic solid wood furnishings. Devil is one of the most popular sites in Bled. It's ideal for some little preparty drinking, although it's not exactly the cheapest so if you want to go intoxicated it may not be your best pick. They provide daily lunch deals and are renowned for hosting strong late-night drinking. The venue draws a highly eclectic population. Another nice thing is that they also provide a fantastic assortment of cigars.

Address: Cesta svobode 15, 4260 Bled, Slovenia

Club Stop

This is the only decent club in Bled, however regrettably it's only available for special occasions. When open, the parties they hold may be extremely fantastic, so it's always good to check out their Facebook for forthcoming events.

Address: Cesta svobode 10, 4260 Bled, Slovenia

Chapter 12

6 DAYS ITINERARY

Day One: Arrival and Allowing Yourself to Relax

- Upon arrival at Lake Bled, go check into the Grand Hotel Toplice, where you will be staying for a magnificent stay.
- Take a stroll down the lakeside promenade and have a delicious lunch at Vila Bled, which offers breathtaking views of the lake.
- In the evening, take some time to relax and rejuvenate at Živa Wellness by indulging in a spa session or savoring a delicious supper by the lakeside at Okarina Bled.

Day two: You will visit Bled Castle and Adventure Park.

- In the morning, enjoy a guided tour of Bled Castle, browse its museum, and take in the breathtaking views from beyond the horizon.
- During the afternoon, you may go on an exciting experience at the Experience Park Bled, where you can do zip-lining and treetop excursions.
- In the evening, dine at Ostarija Peglez'n, which is known for its warm atmosphere and the local delights it serves.

Day Three: Activities in the Great Outdoors

- In the morning, you will go to Bled Island using a traditional pletna boat, ascend the steps, and raise the wishing bell.
- Afternoon: Enjoy water activities at Bled's Watersports Center, featuring paddleboarding and kayaking.
- Evening: Indulge in a lakeside supper at 1906 Bled or Vrtnarija Bled for a sample of Slovenian cuisine.

Day Four: Cultural Exploration

- Morning: Immerse yourself in local art at Bled Gallery and visit exhibitions.
- Afternoon: Discover the natural splendor of Vintgar Gorge with its wooden walkways.
- Evening: Enjoy supper at Old Cellar Bled, recognized for its historic charm and Slovenian cuisine.

Day Five: Nature Walks and Photography

- Morning: Hike around Lake Bled, discovering paths like Ojstrica for spectacular perspectives.
- Afternoon: Capture the beauty of Bled at classic shooting places like Osojnica.
- Evening: Relax with a sunset boat cruise offered by Lake Bled Boats.

Day Six: Relaxation and Departure

- Morning: Leisurely breakfast at the hotel or Lakeside Restaurant and Café.

- Afternoon: Pamper yourself at Vila Bled's spa facilities or take a last stroll around the lakeside.
- Evening: Departure or prolong your stay, departing Lake Bled with wonderful memories.

Safety and Emergency Information at Lake Bled

Emergency Services: -Emergency Number: Dial 112 for general emergencies, including police, medical aid, and fire services.

- Police: Dial 113 for non-emergency police help.
- Medical Assistance: The general emergency number (112) may link you to medical assistance. Hospitals and medical facilities are accessible in adjacent towns including Bled and Radovljica.
- Healthcare: - Medical services in Slovenia are of a good grade. Pharmacies (Lekarna) are accessible for minor health issues, and pharmacists may give guidance.

- European Health Insurance Card (EHIC) holders may obtain required healthcare, however, it's suggested to get travel insurance for supplementary coverage.

Safety Tips:

Natural Hazards:

- Pay attention to weather predictions, particularly if engaged in outside activities. Lake Bled's environs may experience dramatic weather fluctuations.
- Be careful near the water, and observe safety recommendations for water-based activities.

Traffic and Transportation: -

- Slovenia has well-maintained highways, but use care, particularly on small or curving routes. Follow traffic restrictions and be mindful of local driving customs while renting a car.
- Use marked crosswalks while walking and be aware of bikers.

Crime: -

- Slovenia is typically safe, however, practice common sense. Keep valuables protected and remain attentive in busy areas. - Be careful of pickpockets, particularly in tourist sites.

Health Precautions:-

- Stay hydrated, particularly during outdoor activity.
- Use sunscreen to defend against the sun, especially in summer.

Emergency lodgings: -

- Hotels and lodgings in Lake Bled may give aid in case of emergencies. - Keep contact information for your accommodation readily accessible.

Travel Insurance: -

- Consider obtaining travel insurance that covers medical emergencies, trip cancellations, and other unexpected circumstances.

Local Authorities: -

- Familiarize yourself with the location of the local police station, hospital, and emergency services.

While Lake Bled is a safe place, being knowledgeable of emergency protocols and local resources assists in a seamless and happy trip experience. Always emphasize your safety and well-being throughout your stay.

Basic Phrases

1. Hello:Zdravo
2. Goodbye:Nasvidenje
3. Please: Prosim
4. Thank you:Hvala
5. Excuse me / I'm sorry: Oprostite
6. Yes: Da
7. No: Ne
8. How are you?: Kako ste?
9. What is your name?:Kako vam je ime?
10. My name is...:Moje ime je...
11. Nice to meet you: Vesel me je
12. Good morning:Dobro jutro

13. Good afternoon: Dober dan

14. Good evening: Dober večer

15. Good night: Lahko noč

16. How much is this?: Koliko to Stane?

17. Where is...?: Kje je...?

18. I don't understand: Ne razumem

19. Can you assist me?: Mi lahko pomagate?

20. I need...: Potrebujem...

21. I'm lost: Izgubil(a) sem se

22. Excuse me, where is the restroom?: Oprostite, kje je stranišče?

23. Do you speak English?: Govorite angleško?

24. I adore Lake Bled: Obožujem Blejsko jezero

25. What time is it?: Koliko je ura?

26. Good luck: Srečno

27. Cheers!: Na zdravje!

28. I would like...: Rad(a) bi...

29. Where can I locate a taxi?: Kje lahko najdem taksi?

30. Have a wonderful day: Lep dan želim

Conclusion

A Captivating Journey at Lake Bled

Lake Bled, nestled in the embrace of Slovenia's Julian Alps, is a refuge of calm and charm. From the renowned Bled Island to the historic Bled Castle, each moment develops like a beloved chapter in a fairy tale. The symphony of nature, the echoes of folklore, and the warmth of Slovenian hospitality make Lake Bled a destination that transcends seasons. Whether enjoying outdoor experiences or relishing gastronomic pleasures, Lake Bled provides a timeless escape—one that stays in the spirit, generating memories that survive well beyond the borders of its crystal-clear waters.

Printed in Great Britain
by Amazon